C000254056

Jimmy Forsyth

Keith Pattison

Jimmy Forsyth, July 1990, in his flat at The Cedars.

Jimmy Forsyth

Photographs
from the
1950s and 1960s

Selected and with an introduction

by

Anthony Flowers

Tyne Bridge Publishing
in association with Tyne & Wear Archives

Acknowledgements

Tyne Bridge Publishing and Anthony Flowers would like to thank Liz Rees, Chief Archivist, Tyne & Wear Archives; Derek Smith; Peter Scott, the Side Gallery; Juan Fitzgerald; Keith Pattison; Des Walton; Carol Johnstone; Mary Evans.

Photographs ©Jimmy Forsyth unless otherwise credited.
Text ©Anthony Flowers, 2009

ISBN 978 1 85795 133 2

Published by
City of Newcastle upon Tyne
Newcastle Libraries
Tyne Bridge Publishing
2009

www.newcastle.gov.uk

www.tynebridgepublishing.co.uk

All rights reserved. No part of this book may be reproduced, stored or introduced into a retrieval system, or transmitted in any form or by any means (electronic, mechanical, photocopying, recording or otherwise) without the prior permission of the publishers.

British Library Cataloguing in Publication data: a catalogue record for this book is available from the British Library.

Printed by Elanders UK Ltd., North Tyneside

'Mr James Forsyth Esq. on roof of Tulloch Street Hall (St Stephens) prior to its demolition. View 1960.'

Wherever possible we have used Jimmy Forsyth's original captions to the photographs, and these appear in quotes.

Where there is no caption, we have been unable to identify the subject or the date.

Park Road, 1959.

Introduction

These remarkable photographs of a vanished Tyneside were taken between 1954 and 1967 by a long-term unemployed man who lived, during this time, on the Scotswood Road in the west end of Newcastle upon Tyne. They represent what has been recognised as one of the most important records of twentieth-century working-class society that anyone has produced. Considering the circumstances under which they were taken, it is remarkable that they have survived at all. That man was Jimmy Forsyth.

Jimmy Forsyth was born to John and Bertha Forsyth, on 15 August 1913, at 24 Trinity Street in Barry, an industrial town in South Wales built on the rich coalfields of Glamorganshire. It had been the major exporter of coal until the Great Western Railway extended its reach to Cardiff. For Jimmy, Barry was a fascinating fusion of the rural, marine and industrial. It was, in fact, not unlike his eventual adoptive Tyneside.

The Forsyths came from Garmouth, not far from the mouth of the Spey in Elgin, north-east Scotland. Jimmy's grandfather, James, was a stonemason. Like his grandson would, he too walked to find work, making his way to Liverpool and then to Bangor in North Wales, where Jimmy's father, John, was born in 1881. Eventually James was to find work in the docks of Barry and Cardiff.

When Jimmy was born he was not expected to live, and remained a slight child with a pronounced cast to his left eye. He went to High Street School, Barry, and left at 14, without formal qualifications. On leaving school, he became an apprentice fitter in a cement works repair shop. Jimmy successfully gained his apprenticeship in 1934 but he found it hard to get regular work. At his father's suggestion he joined the Merchant Navy. He went to Newport and signed on as an assistant engineer, eventually rising to fourth engineer, on board several ships throughout 1936 and 1937.

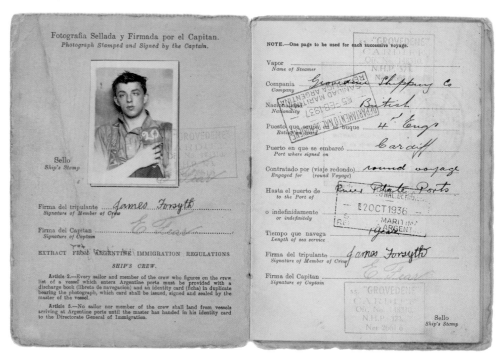

His career as a merchant seaman, seems to have come to an abrupt end on 26 August 1937 when he signed off from the SS *St Helena* at Sunderland and returned to Wales. In 1938 he went to work, under the Ministry of Supply, on the construction of a small arms factory owned by ICI at Hirwaun near Merthyr

Tydfil. He learned that fitters were required in Mossend, Glasgow, so he volunteered along with three workmates. By 1940, with the Second World War well underway, he returned to Merthyr.

Jimmy Forsyth arrived in Newcastle from South Wales, aged thirty, in 1943. He found a room in Grove Street, Elswick just off the Scotswood Road. He had come to work as a fitter at ICI in Prudhoe, a short train journey west along the the Tyne. As a volunteer in Merthyr he had agreed to come north for a period of three months to help with the frantic effort to maintain munitions for the war. Tragically, he was at ICI for just four days before an accident, while he was working on a boiler, left him blind in his right eye – a metal splinter from a broken chisel tore into his pupil. After a period of convalescence in a hospital at Wylam, in the Tyne Valley, he returned to Elswick to find that his room had been re-let, and a workmate's family at Crawcrook, a few miles from Gateshead, offered him lodgings. Despite his accident he returned to work. In 1945 he moved to Prudhoe, on the south bank of the Tyne, while continuing at ICI, but the eventual return of employees from the demobilising forces created tensions. Things came to a head late in 1946 when a dispute with a foreman led to his dismissal. He was still keen to stay on Tyneside and decided to remain temporarily in Prudhoe, though his disability had significantly reduced his chances of employment.

In 1946, with rationing still on and little prospect of work, Jimmy needed to find cheaper lodgings. He landed up in what he described as a 'half-brothel' in Suffolk Street, Elswick. He survived there in these unusual circumstances until 1951, but by 1952 he had found a Tyneside flat on the Scotswood Road.

Most of Jimmy's time was taken up with the search for a job and without the money for bus or train fares, the daylight hours were spent walking from place to place in the hope of employment. The dole was usually £2 but if you said that you lived in digs you got more. The search for work took him to London,

Reading, Manchester and Nottingham then to Canterbury and London again before returning to Tyneside, only to be told by the Labour Exchange at Manors in Newcastle that he was no longer eligible for the dole. These were difficult times.

He eventually found temporary work as a cleaner in the kitchens of the Station Hotel. A handyman's job at an ironworks across the river near Blaydon ended in near disaster when a crane jib struck him, fracturing his skull. Jimmy's independent spirit and forthright nature did not make him an easy employee so he attempted self-employment in 1955, when he took on a general dealer's shop in Pine Street, Elswick, financed it is said by compensation for the accident. However this was no more successful, as he gave too much credit to his customers.

In exactly which year Jimmy first acquired a camera is uncertain. Some photographs that appear in his tartan albums (photograph albums with a distinctive tartan cover that Jimmy used to contain his earliest work) seem to predate the demolition of Newcastle's Old Infirmary in 1954, which provided Jimmy with the impetus to begin recording places that were disappearing. It is important not to underestimate what an undertaking this was to become for an unemployed man with few resources, though he said that by selling prints to his neighbours he was able to manage.

A natural curiosity about the history of the city, also led to him making exposures of interesting buildings. The tartan albums began to contain, alongside pictures of friends and their children, views of places he had visited, parts of the surviving Town Walls, supposed Roman remains; almost anything that looked historic seemed to require a photograph and appropriate caption. 'View look[ing] west up Neville Street – note; island absent from up road centre as it has not been laid', or in a more historical vein 'Southern Postern gateway – note; believed to be [the] only completely preserved Norman postern in England.'

1954

HORSES AT CRAWCROOK   COUNTY DURHAM
1954

Nº 1   Nº 2   Nº 3

VIEWS OF OLD INFIRMARY DURING DISMANTLING
AUTUMN 1954
(Note:- No 1 shows small digger with wire
fastend through window No 2 collapse
of wall Nº 3 Work that was accomplished)

A detached page from the first of Jimmy's tartan albums showing the dismantling of the old Infirmary in the autumn of 1954

On the night of December 23-24 1955 the Tyne Tees Coaster, *Cyprian Coast* sank in the Tyne between the Newcastle and Gateshead quaysides. It had previously been in collision with a Swedish ship *Arabert* and sank within five minutes, the ten-man crew having had a remarkable escape. Jimmy, obviously attracted by this dramatic maritime subject, returned many times to record the salvage operation during the months of January and February 1956.

A more sustained period of employment saw Jimmy working as part of a Trinidad Lake asphalting team. Even when supposed to be labouring he took a sequence of photographs of workmates as they replaced roads south of the river in County Durham.

He was taking pictures of local children when a neighbour told him that Scotswood Road, and the surrounding area, was to be demolished, and suggested he make a record of where he lived. It was the perfect subject – combining history and the gritty reality of what had become an extremely rundown working-class area. An indication of how systematic he was to become in his recording of Scotswood Road is evident in a sequence of photographs taken in 1956 along the road from Churchill Street to Park Road, Park Road to Rendell Street, and Rendell Street to School Street. He went on to photograph the remainder of the area over the next three years. In fact, such is the entirety of his record that when Newcastle Libraries came to make a book on the forty or so Scotswood Road pubs, many of which had disappeared by 1988, they were able to source the illustrations largely from Jimmy's photographs.

The next five years were to be a time of almost feverish activity for Jimmy. During these years he produced the majority of his most memorable and remarkable images.

In the mid 1950s Jimmy came to know a local photographer, Steve Wood. Steve was manager of Turner's Photographic Dealers shop at 62 Clayton Street. Steve Wood thought Jimmy had been attracted by photographs of old Newcastle he had taken, which were displayed in the shop window. In any case they had much in common, a passion for local history and Jimmy's growing interest in photography. Jimmy was often in the shop telling Steve of the impending demolition of local landmarks: 'He used to tell me all about the pubs and buildings of note that were being pulled down … I would make a note of these so that I could include them on my Sunday morning forays'. Jimmy showed him prints that he had taken, and Steve would give him film, 'then I would tell him to bring the film in when he had finished it.

'Old Newcastle Infirmary corner of Railway St & Scotswood Rd. Taken in Railway St. June 1954.'

If there was anything I wanted, I would keep the print,' from which Steve would make a transparency for use in slideshows he put on in the area. The relationship developed, though Steve could find Jimmy's presence in the shop distracting, and encouraged him to choose slack periods for his visits. 'Jimmy was not in the market for buying things, and I think I kept him in films at first. Then I had a sale in the shop, where I offered five shillings for any old camera, regardless of state, in part-exchange. It does not seem much, does it? But this was the 1950s. I just put them all in a bin, and let Jimmy when he came in, pick out anything he was interested in. The rest were packed in a box for the bin men.' It was Steve who offered Jimmy a twenty-year-old Rolleiflex camera for £15, which was a huge sum

'View up Gloucester Street.'

'View along Oak Street eastwards from Gloucester Street of Andrew Beveridge aged 4 1960.'

of money for a man on the dole. He was allowed to pay off the purchase price in instalments.

Although Jimmy has always denied anything but a rudimentary acquaintance with photographic technique, it is difficult not to conclude that Steve Wood gave Jimmy much practical advice with regards to exposure and instruction in the use of flash for interiors. When Jimmy's father died in 1960 Steve Wood gave him one of his old suits and a shirt to wear for the funeral (he was told by Steve's wife to polish the shoes he was wearing). His train fare to Barry was covered by a discretionary grant from National Assistance.

'Jimmy knew Scotswood like a book, and was a treasure of information' and, as Steve Wood was to discover, he had considerable knowledge of Newcastle's history. 'Well, whilst I was in his house, he took a key and opened a bedroom door. Here on shelves there were racks of tomes, by all the best-known [local] historians, Bourne, McKenzie, Welford, Charleton and many others. He had a fortune tied up there ... I asked where he got them. Oh, he said, he saved up and used to go to Stedemans [Robert D. Steedman, a well known antiquarian dealer] at the bottom of Grey Street and buy them, or put them aside, till he could. As he would only be on Assistance allowance, he must have starved himself to buy them'. In a blue Monarch exercise book, Jimmy recorded the contents of his personal library, which at that time was approaching three hundred volumes covering a variety of subjects: autobiographies and biographies; the study of language and dictionaries; an extensive section devoted to works about Scotland (Jimmy has always been immensely proud of his Scottish roots); atlases and a number of periodicals, many of which were of antiquarian interest and of considerable value. It has not been possible to establish what happened to them.

Eventually, Jimmy's flat, too, was swept away by the developers. As the condemned houses were demolished and the land was cleared for the new flats to house displaced families, the developers had to keep one step ahead. Jimmy followed the progress with his camera, driven by a compulsion to get things down simply and quickly: 'You don't think that things are going to change that quick, you believe some things will be there for ever'. This urgency is captured in Jimmy's description of one such photographic assignment: 'Mary Rutherford had a second-hand shop along here, I looked down into the

'*View along Scotswood Road across Myrtle Terrace. My house is fourth door along from Falcon Motors shop (a new business). View in 1956.*'

Rolleiflex as the digger started like, and when I looked up there was nothing to be seen, down it fell, it had gone in a cloud of dust.' Eventually those left behind wanted to move as the dust, disruption, the vermin and the opportunist thieves made life impossible. Jimmy moved to Woodland Crescent on a 1930s estate off Delaval Road. With this move he was now in the heart of an area that was to become notorious in the 1960s for the Mary Bell murders.

In 1964 Jimmy began documenting the demolition of another important landmark, the old Scotswood Bridge (Scotswood Suspension Bridge). This was to be a lengthy project, as it was not until 1967, after the opening of the replacement bridge, that it was finally removed. At night he worked as a watchman on a sheltered housing development near Benwell, and by day he watched and recorded the progress of the contractors. In 1971 he moved again, to a house in Forest Road, which he shared with friends from his early years on Scotswood Road.

'Mrs Mary Rutherford secondhand shop on Scotswood Road. She feeds the pigeons left by people who have been rehoused. 1960.'

'View in Tea Company shop at foot of Suffolk Street 1958.'

'Demolition work in Pine Street of south side between Maple and Ivy Streets, Sept 8th 1960.'

'Mr Kern and his lorry, demolition work Pine Street. Left rear is part of Kyle Street. October 4th 1960.'

Throughout the late 1960s and well into the 1970s Jimmy seems to have used several cameras. Most notably there is the gradual introduction of colour into his photography. He had taken some colour pictures in the 1950s but these were for special occasions – parties or weddings. The high cost of colour film was obviously an important consideration, which prevented him from exploiting its special qualities more frequently. The colour work from the 1970s has not worn well and many prints contained in albums in Tyne & Wear Archives are in poor condition. Jimmy's rather erratic and haphazard methods of storage have not helped. The same subjects are in evidence but it has to be said that few from this period, have the visual interest of his earlier work. He nevertheless continued to record all the major construction projects that took place during those years, including the construction of the Western Bypass and the development of Eldon Square into a modern shopping centre.

For a long time Jimmy's photographs remained largely hidden from public view and few people had any idea of his ongoing project. In 1956 Desmond Walton, a librarian based in the west of the city, met Jimmy in Elswick. 'I didn't realise at the time that he was taking photographs. The only clue I had was that I saw Jimmy standing on Park Road with a camera in his hand talking to some people.' Eventually, however, in 1974 'Jimmy came in out of the blue with his albums, all the tiny contact prints of work going back to 1954 right up to the present day. I was absolutely staggered to see what he had done – it was a systematic approach with a proper index. Finally, he asked if he could leave the negative albums with me at the library because he was afraid that if anything happened to him they might be thrown out and destroyed. No one would understand their value.' Recognising the significance of what Jimmy had shown him, Des arranged for prints to be made from the negatives and mounted a number of exhibitions. The response to these exhibitions from local people was enthusiastic, prompting an outpouring of memories. Des began to interview and collect stories in an attempt to gain an understanding of the area, and of the people who lived there. This material is now housed in West End Library at West Newcastle Local Studies and has become a substantial archive of memories and documentary material.

In 1981 Newcastle's innovative Side Gallery brought Jimmy's work to a wider public. Derek Smith (himself a fine photographer, film maker and researcher) spent many hours uncovering Jimmy's story, arranging for exhibition prints to be made from the negatives, and patiently transcribing Jimmy's often extensive captions. This exhibition created enormous interest, and demand for publication in book form grew. The publication of *Scotswood Road* in 1986 by Bloodaxe Books coincided with an expanded exhibition of Jimmy's photographs at the Side Gallery. This was followed by the Tyne Tees Television documentary *No Fancy Shades*. In 1987 Jimmy received the Halina Award for Photography, travelling to London to collect his award. Recognition has brought its rewards. Jimmy's work has found its way into mixed exhibitions across the country, and many articles about him, have appeared in local and national newspapers and magazines. The media attention and his constant presence on the city streets during the 1980s helped Jimmy acquire something of a folk status on Tyneside. The film director Mike Figgis cast him as a newspaper seller in his 1988 feature film *Stormy Monday*. More bizarrely, Jimmy was invited with his cameras and albums of photographs to the studios of Tyne Tees Television, to be interviewed live on the rock and pop programme *The Tube*. Although Jimmy's celebrity status gradually meant that the business of making street portraits and recording a changing Newcastle became easier (he was to receive significant royalties for the *Scotswood Road* book, which was a local best seller), the remarkable achievements of the 1950s and 60s were never matched.

In 1983 Jimmy moved from Forest Road to a high-rise block, The Cedars, off Park Road. It was almost full circle to this part of Scotswood Road, where he had arrived forty years before. The move brought very mixed feelings, as he remained sceptical about the motives of the planners with their preference for this form of housing. As he caustically remarked 'planners unfortunately never live in their constructions or they would be more careful. High rise flats for instance are only makeshift establishments, cannot and never will compare to a house of one's own and communities cannot naturally exist in such conditions. Living here I know about only eight or nine of the ninety or so people who live here. All on my floor are new, as you go out you meet in the lift, not as in a street where you pass people on doorsteps. Nobody stands at the flat door and you are too quickly away to see anyone. IF I HAD MY WAY I WOULD BLOW THEM ALL UP.'

After a number of years, concerns about his declining mobility led to him being relocated to a flat nearer ground level, sadly without the views that he cherished.

By the early 1990s, Jimmy, now in his late seventies, was increasingly vulnerable. In 1992 he returned to Barry. The award of a Northern Arts travel bursary, allowed him to make the trip with local journalist Veronica Johnson who first met Jimmy in the early 1980s. She had become a close friend and was preparing to write his biography, but tragically this was to remain unrealised as Veronica died suddenly in 1999. Jimmy hoped that this trip

'View from Byron Terrace of High Flats Scotswood Road. Left to right are the Willows, the Beeches & the Poplars. House at top of Byron Street is used by Birds Builder, background De Gray Street, July 21st 1961.'

Famous Elswick Sausages
'Butchers & General Dealers shop,
Westmorland Road.'

'Looking East
along Scotswood
Road from Frank
Street showing
newsagents shop.
1956.'

to his birthplace, would give him an opportunity to take photographs, which could be used in the proposed biography. In Barry, Jimmy was drawn to the docks and railway sidings where his father had worked. In the evening, Veronica and Jimmy, were entertained 'by members of the railway club'. Veronica contacted High Street School and they made Jimmy guest of honour for the day. Delighted by the response of the pupils and teachers, he left copies of *Scotswood Road* in the school library. The next day *The Barry and District News* ran a feature on the return journey and Jimmy's work as a documentary photographer. Sadly, he was unable to trace any surviving relatives. His mother had died in 1958, his father in 1960 and afterwards he had lost contact with his half-brother John; it seems that he too had died just before the trip. As part of the journey had been to search for lost relatives, Jimmy was visibly moved on his return to Tyneside having found no one from his generation still in Barry.

Declining health from 2000 onwards meant that Jimmy was largely confined to his flat at The Cedars. The days of wandering were finally over. His appetite for taking photographs remained undiminished as he fired off shots of visitors with his Olympus Trip camera. There is also a series of photographs of images taken from his wide screen television.

The days now were spent reading (aided by a large magnifying glass). Appropriately, he particularly enjoyed travel writing 'older ones preferably'. He was fascinated by accounts of the sinking of the *Titanic*. Unable to get to libraries he made full use of the contacts he had made over the years, with requests for increasingly obscure books. Although he never married (rumours of romantic attachments persist) he always had several dedicated friends who helped him to maintain his independence. After a series of falls it became clear that he could no longer look after himself, and he was moved to a care home. Initially he was taken on trips to the Grainger Market, the quayside and the Baltic Centre for Contemporary Art (where he expressed his opinions on the exhibitions forcibly).

'View up Norfolk Street back lane towards Cambridge Street seen in background. 1961'

'Fire at W. Prendergast's of Sycamore Street west of Gloucester Street 1959.'

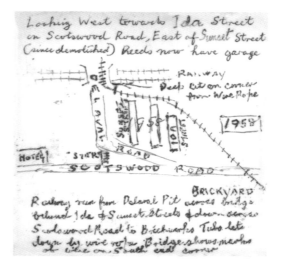

Scotswood Road. On the reverse of the photograph are Jimmy's detailed notes including in this case a small sketch map of the area.

'*Looking West towards Ida Street on Scotswood Road, East of Sunset Street (since demolished) Reeds now have garage … 1958.*

Railway ran from Delaval Pit across bridge behind Ida & Sunset Streets & down across Scotswood Road to Brickworks. Tubs let down by wire rope. Bridge shows marks of wire on South end corner.'

'*View off west side of Redheugh Bridge showing lead works & its Shot Tower (was last remaining in England now demolished). Also gas tank to right of Shot Tower of Elswick Gas Company. August 22nd 1960.*'

'*View of old & new Scotswood Bridge from South showing stairs used as temporary way onto New Bridge. April 2nd 1967.*'

Eventually it became clear that he found these outings an ordeal and he remains, at the time of writing, largely within the confines of the home.

In 2002 while researching for Tyne Bridge Publishing's book, *Out of One Eye*, Derek Smith interviewed some of the children, now adults, who had appeared in Jimmy's photographs. They provided some remarkable memories of life along the Scotswood Road. It is rare for the subject of a photograph to get a right of reply, to describe the circumstances under which it was taken and why. Pat Logan proudly held up an original print (extremely creased and with areas of the print surface missing) of the photograph Jimmy had taken of her and her friend Pat Norman in 1957 (see page 73). 'We'd been to a shop in Suffolk Street for chews and just come round the corner into Sycamore Street. We came across Jimmy and he said, "Just stand there and I'll take your photos."' She has kept this battered print of herself as a child, in every handbag she has ever owned.

Placing Jimmy's photographs in a gallery context changes them; we see them differently. Mick Bidewell, responding to an article about Jimmy in *Amateur Photographer*, wrote that 'thanks to Jimmy's decision to record what was around him while it was still there, I can revisit the very location where – aged five – I crashed my pedal car, resulting in a bump on the head on which my mum resorted to the rather dubious cure of rubbing it with a knob of butter.' This association of the personal with the inconsequential, the easily overlooked with the dispassionate record of appearance, gives the photographs a life way beyond the circumstances of their taking.

We can come back to the topographic views and attempt to reconstruct the position of a building or the course of a road but we cannot place individuals in the same way, they have moved on with their lives. At such a distance in time, it is also impossible to place Jimmy within his photographs; occasionally his shadow intrudes, but he is mostly missing. There are a few photographs where he appears

'Bells Timber Yard fire & an old fire engine. Site: junction of Forth & Railway Streets 1959.'

'Here we have a hole in the bedroom of a house in Pine Street. A beer wagon from the Hope and Anchor Brewery ran backwards across the road into this lady's house. They used that in the Chronicle, though I didn't get much for it, 7s 6d'

(Scotswood Road, Bloodaxe Books, 1986.)

as a part of the scene, usually in the background. an elusive presence that states that he was there, a witness concerned with photographing history.

In Tyne & Wear Archives there is a substantial collection of albums, negative files, cardboard boxes brimming with seemingly endless folders of processed films, documents of his life, letters and royalty statements for the *Scotswood Road* book. They are being catalogued and conserved. It is a daunting task, as much that has survived is understandably in poor condition. Jimmy seems never to have decided what to keep and what to discard, preferring to leave those decisions to posterity. Obviously, things have been lost during the many moves, and doubtless negatives and photographs will have been borrowed and never returned. Jimmy remarked philosophically 'It's no good burying the pictures. They should be given out to more people, and they should be free, after all they belong to their subjects, to the people themselves'.

Jimmy's generosity of spirit is admirable, and his photographs have been extensively reproduced over the years. A 1960 photograph of the hole in the bedroom wall of a house in Pine Street, after a runaway beer wagon from the Hope and Anchor brewery ran backwards, was taken up by the *Evening Chronicle* 'though I didn't get much for it, 7s 6d', is an early example of Jimmy's work reaching a wide audience. At times the classic images can seem over familiar, lessening their impact. While it is the images of mainly working-class people that have been most reproduced, Jimmy's subject matter is more far-reaching and varied. The later colour work indicates that he sought out aspects of Tyneside that reflected his changed circumstances, and at the present moment we are not sufficiently removed from them to judge their worth.

Jimmy's was not a nostalgic vision, filled with regret or a deep sense of loss, it was rather the result of a profound concern to fix forever that which he knew. These remarkable photographs are a unique record of a part of Tyneside that once existed and is no more. There is something intensely engaging in the way in which he had an instant rapport with his subjects; they seem completely at ease, comfortable in his presence. The intimacy of these photographs is a rare and wonderful achievement, because they represent a vanished community seen and photographed from within.

'View of Ebenezer Chapel (1863) on west side of Rendel Street (Cushy Butterfield nearabouts on same site). May 1956.'

Select bibliography

Scotswood Road, Jimmy Forsyth, ed. Derek Smith, Bloodaxe Books 1986.

Looking back at Scotswood Road Pubs, Newcastle upon Tyne City Libraries and Arts 1988.

Old Scotswood Road, A. Desmond Walton with West Newcastle Local Studies, Chalford, 1997.

'Little Brother is Watching You', Gordon Burn, *The Guardian Weekend Magazine*, 30th June 2001.

Out of One Eye The Photography of Jimmy Forsyth, Anthony Flowers and Derek Smith, Tyne Bridge Publishing 2002.

In addition to the published material on Jimmy I have made extensive use of the albums and documents from Jimmy's personal collection in Tyne & Wear Archives and the following:

Jimmy Forsyth Metro Radio interview recorded at the Side Gallery October 7, 1986, (unpublished tape recording); 'Lives through a Lens' a BBC *Close Up North* film (broadcast in 2001); 'Jimmy Forsyth of Elswick, Newcastle upon Tyne – My Life', November 1989, (unpublished autograph manuscript); Jimmy Forsyth interviewed by Les Bell at West Newcastle Local Studies February 7, 1995, (unpublished tape recording); Jimmy Forsyth interviewed by Derek Smith (in preparation for *Out of One Eye*) 2001, (unpublished tape recordings); Mary Evans for background material on Jimmy's family and his early life in Barry (personal correspondence with the author 2008-9).

The photographs used in the introduction and on pages 5 and 33 are reproduced (reduced in size) from original prints of the 1950s and 1960s, and are taken from Jimmy's albums. Most of them are annotated on the back.

Jimmy Forsyth at Tyne & Wear Archives

Tyne & Wear Archives Service began acquiring Jimmy Forsyth's extensive archive in the early 1990s when a grant from Northern Arts enabled the purchase of a large collection of material that Jimmy had already begun depositing in the archives. This included original prints of what is probably Jimmy's best work, dating from the 1950s and early 60s, contained in the so-called 'tartan albums', as well as huge numbers of later colour photographs and negatives. Over the years Jimmy regularly added to this body of work and visited weekly to help identify the subjects of his photographs.

It was not until 2001 that the archives service acquired the original negatives of the early work, which had previously been lodged at the West Newcastle Local Studies Library in Benwell, as well as copies of contact prints from these made by that collection's volunteer group. The survival of the negatives for future generations is therefore assured.

More recently the archive has been further enhanced by more original early pictures that Jimmy had kept at his home, and these have now been fully conserved so that both the prints and Jimmy's original notes on the back can be easily viewed.

Sorting and fully cataloguing this huge archive will take many years, but in the meantime parts of it can be accessed and copies for personal use can be ordered from Tyne & Wear Archives Service. Copyright in the collection is retained by Jimmy Forsyth during his lifetime.

Liz Rees, Tyne & Wear Archives
March 2009

'Left to right Sandy Skinner and Fred Farmer, 1958.'

'Gatters McElderry' c.1957.

'Used car site. Water Street Scotswood Road. Maurice Wilson & workmen.'

'Electricians in Delaval Road during demolition for continuation westwards of Whitehaven Road. 1961.'

'Old Man at Quayside.'

Railway bridge, Gateshead High Street, 1960.

'Castle curator Newcastle on Tyne.'

'Jimmy the Cooper and Mr Bryson, 1958.'

'Charles Francis Knife and scissor grinder, 1958.'

'Mr Moore – Robinson's bookstore.' [Sidney Moore was manager.]

'North East corner of site for Kings Meadow & Houghton Court flats. Budle Street is in background running up from Wokingham Street. 1959.'

'Asphalt Men at New Silksworth. September 1956.'

'Asphalting of Road at Windy Nook Sept 1956.'

Road repairs in County Durham, 1956.

'Hawkers in backlane between Scotswood Road and Penn Street, April 1957.'

'*Isaac Stuart a tatter or rag-man in Delaval Road just below Forest Road, w. Benwell (Note the cobble road & houses since removed in 1978), 1959.*'

'*Waites Family Delaval Road.*'

'*These were tallymen collecting in the Gloucester Street area for the ticket shops.*'

The Quayside, St George's Day, 1958.

'Saturday morning market, Quayside.'

'Young men about town.' 1957.

'Valerie Findlay at Town Moor 30th June 1958.'

'*Yolande Gladders on Vic's Housey-Housey Stall June 30th 1958.*'

The Long Sands, Tynemouth, August Bank Holiday, 1955.

'Children in Leazes Park, April 1957.'

Gibson's shop, 1958.

'Peggy [Moore] and grandchildren in shop.'

'Nancy Little with husband (centre) and baby.' 1956.

'*Jackie Prendergast, 1956.*'

Blaydon Races Centenary celebrations, June 1962.

'*Mullins family Suffolk Street 1957.*'

Ralph Liddle c1958.

'*Robert Foster and Linda Gladders.*'

'Brownies July 26th 1958. Maureen Beveridge & Carol.'

'Stuart & Andrew Beveridge.'

The street corner studio. A sequence of photographs taken on January 2, 1958.

'Stephen Charlton Jan 2nd 1958.'

The Royal Oak, Scotswood Road, 1956.

Pat Norman and Pat Logan, Sycamore Street, 1957.

Maureen Beveridge, Sycamore Street, 1958.

Anne Prendergast outside the Gloucester pub, Gloucester Street, 1957.

'*Nancy Bates with Ralph & Shirley Ann, Laurel Street.*'

'*Dorothy & Carol & Arthur Bransby July 26th 1958.*'

1956.

'*Thomas and Johnny Short.*'

'Betty Young & relatives.'

Charlie Airey, Delaval Road, 1958.

'Edith Jardine.'

'Eric Charlton's girlfriend Gloucester Street 1954.'

1957

Goucester Street, 1957.

'Yolande Gladders.'

Scotswood Road, 1960.

'Scene of crash in Scotswood Road (between Motor Cycle & Car). August 28th 1958.
Ambulance arriving at scene of crash.'

'View down Clara Street from Buddle Road. 1955'

'May 1960. Cruddas Park Flats on Site of St Vincents School Home.'

Tank, Gloucester Arms, January 1957.

Near East Street, July 1959.

'View of Green Tree Inn, Scotswood Road.'

From 'Views along Scotswood Road March 10th 1956.'

From 'Views along Scotswood Road March 10th 1956.'

'Hawe Street from south 1956.'

John Wright and Jimmy Bell, the corner of Myrtle Place and Scotswood Road, 1958.

'*Jackie Prendergast [and friend].*'

Singh family, 1958.

'Lily Clift & brother aged 4 months July 1958.'

'Bridget & Baby.'

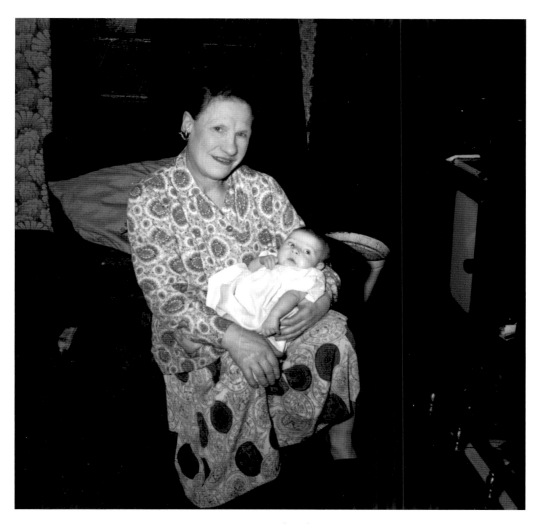

'Lizzie Scott & Baby.'

'View east along Pine Street showing stripping gang taking wood and slates off empty houses. August 24th 1960.'

Pushing down a chimney on Sycamore Street, August 1960.

St Stephen's parish hall, 1960.

Sycamore and Suffolk Street demolition, 1961.

George Street, 1957.

'*Roof of St Stephens Parish hall in Tulloch Street. Left to right: Vic Summers & Edward Turnbull. October 6th 1960.*'

'View from the rear steps of Gloucester Street.'

'View from window lower end of Park Road. Sept 29th 1960.'

'*Junction of Ord Street and Railway Street.*'

Ord Street. 'Main gate at west end Cattle Market with Scotswood Rd on left of photo.
View 1956 July 22nd.'

'View of Scotswood Road in the Snow.'

'Clayton Street 1959.'

'Temple of Atenocitus Benwell' [Temple of Antenociticus, Broomridge Avenue.]

Sailors' Bethel, Horatio Street.

'Quayside. Feb 6th 1956.'

9 February 1956, the wreck of the Cyprian Coast refloated in the Tyne.

Titan II crane removing a smaller crane over River Tyne to cement loading wharf, summer, 1959.

'Sandhill from the Tyne Bridge, 1958.'

Grey Street from Grey's Monument, 1957.

The Royal Arcade, 1960.

Jesmond Dene, 1957.

The road to East Herrington, 7 September 1958.

Castle turret, June 1957.

Castle turret, February 1958.

The Central Station, 1957.

The Keelmen's Hospital, 1954.

Durham Tower, Bath Lane, 7 July, 1959.

Stotes Hall, Jesmond, 1957.

The Bessie Surtees, about to pass under the Swing Bridge, 12 July 1958.

'View North across Tyne W. of London and North East Railway Bridge. The chimneys belonged to Adamzez the famous toilet makers. The Bobbie Shaftoe & its sister ships took ashes from Stella Power Station to be dumped at sea.'

View of Blackett Street from Grey's Monument.

'Another cable cut through Scotswood Bridge May 10th 1967.'

'Winch for hauling cables across river at Old Scotswood Bridge. After they are cut off at south side they are cut on north & drawn out for scrap.'

Scotswood Bridge, 1967.

'*View up Suffolk Street from Scotswood Road. On corner is London & Newcastle Tea Co. shop.*'